Read All About It!

Read All About

THE HUMAN BODY

by Claire Throp

raintree
a Capstone company — publishers for children

Raintree is an imprint of Capstone Global Library Limited, a company incorporated in England and Wales having its registered office at 264 Banbury Road, Oxford, OX2 7DY – Registered company number: 6695582

www.raintree.co.uk
myorders@raintree.co.uk

Edited by Peter Mavrikis
Designed by Kayla Rossow
Original illustrations © Capstone Global Library Limited 2022
Picture research by Morgan Walters
Production by Laura Manthe
Originated by Capstone Global Library Ltd
Printed and bound in India

978 1 3982 2586 2 (hardback)
978 1 3982 2585 5 (paperback)

British Library Cataloguing in Publication Data
A full catalogue record for this book is available from the British Library.

Acknowledgements
We would like to thank the following for permission to reproduce photographs: iStockphoto: Nerthuz, top right 4; Shutterstock: ABIR ROY BARMAN, top 31, adike, bottom 4, Afonkin_Y, top 5, Africa Studio, 22, Billion Photos, top right Cover, BlueRingMedia, top 27, Can Desing, bottom 20, CLIPAREA l Custom media, top 21, David Marchal, top 20, Dean Drobot, top 25, Designua, 14, Emilio100, bottom 25, Evgenyrychko, top 29, Fresnel, bottom 16, Gelpi, top 11, Giovanni Cancemi, top 17, Jemastock, design element throughout, joshya, top 23, kaling2100, bottom left 19, Kelvin Degree, design element throughout, LightField Studios, middle left 15, loocmill, top 26, Magic mine, 12, Maria Samburova, (watercolor) Cover, Martin D. Vonka, bottom 5, Master1305, 1, bottom 1, Monkey Business Images, top 6, Mrkevvzime, bottom 7, naluwan, bottom 26, Nerthuz, 24, NoPainNoGain, bottom 21, Palmer Kane LLC, top 10, Phonlamai Photo, top 7, photka, top 30, pixelheadphoto digitalskillet, bottom Cover, top right 9, Praisaeng, bottom right 19, ReVelStockArt, design element throughout, Rob Marmion, bottom 30, Robert Kneschke, top 15, Rudmer Zwerver, middle left 9, Samuel Borges Photography, 18, sciencepics, bottom 17, SciePro, bottom 9, top 16, bottom 23, stihii, 8, stockaboo, bottom 31, Bottom of Form, Sunisa Butphet, bottom 6, Tarr Pichet, top right 19, travelview, 28, violetblue, 13, VipadaLoveYou, bottom 29, WAYHOME studio, bottom 11, Zurijeta, bottom 27

Every effort has been made to contact copyright holders of material reproduced in this book. Any omissions will be rectified in subsequent printings if notice is given to the publisher.

Contents

Words in **bold** are in the glossary.

Chapter 1

The heart and blood

The heart is a very important muscle. It pumps blood around the body in tubes called blood vessels.

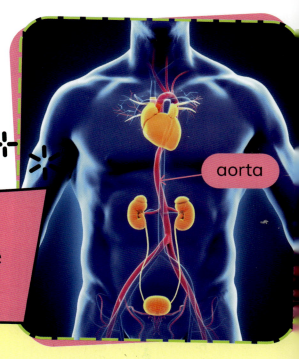

aorta

The biggest blood vessel is the aorta. It is about the same width as your thumb.

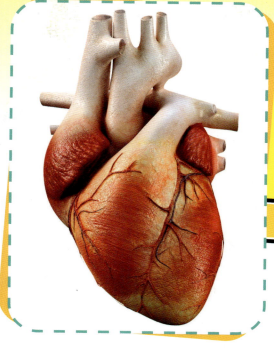

The heart beats about 100,000 times every day!

Each heartbeat pumps about 60 millilitres (4 tablespoons) of blood around the body.

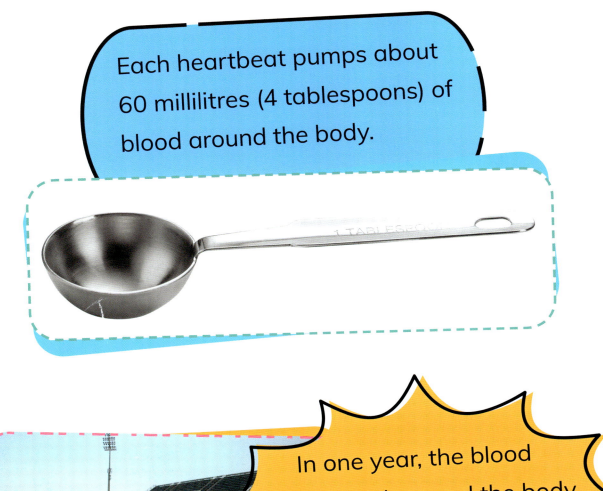

In one year, the blood pumped around the body would fill an Olympic-sized swimming pool.

There are four main blood groups – A, B, AB and O. The most common type is O. 63 per cent of people have blood type O.

We think of blood as being red. But more than half of it is actually yellow. The yellow comes from liquid called **plasma**.

Blood also contains red blood **cells**, white blood cells and **platelets**.

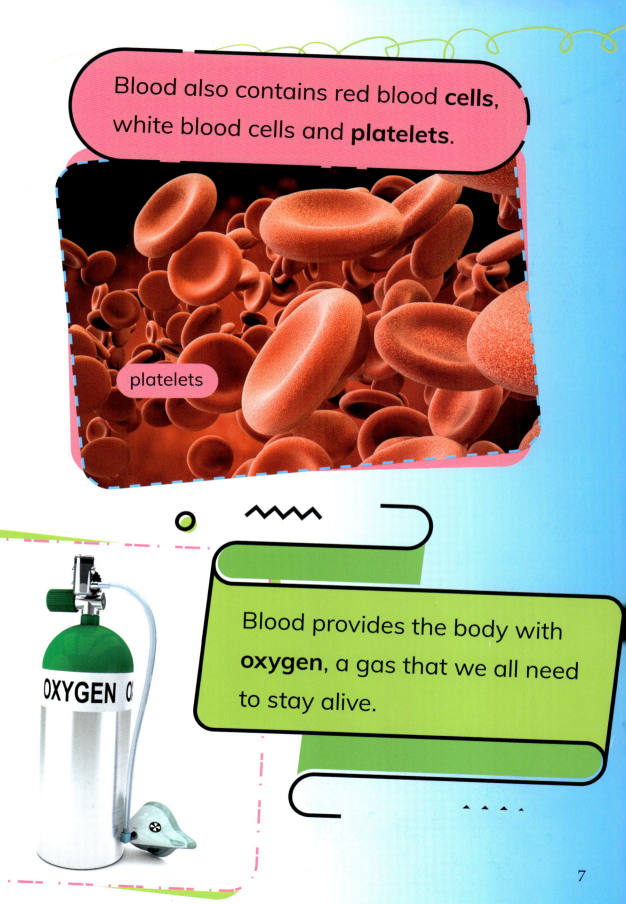

platelets

Blood provides the body with **oxygen**, a gas that we all need to stay alive.

OXYGEN

Chapter 2

Muscles

Muscles help us to stand upright, move and breathe. They are soft and are joined to our hard bones by **tendons**.

There are more than 650 skeletal muscles in the body!

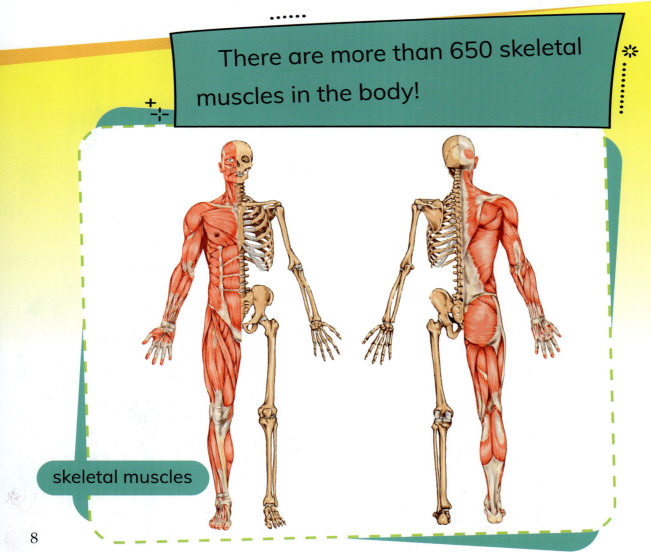

skeletal muscles

Muscles make up about half of a person's body weight.

The word muscle comes from a Latin word, musculus. It means "mouse".

Heart muscles keep our hearts beating. These muscles work without us having to think about it.

9

There are eight muscles in the tongue!

gluteus maximus

The largest muscle in the body is the gluteus maximus. It helps you climb and run.

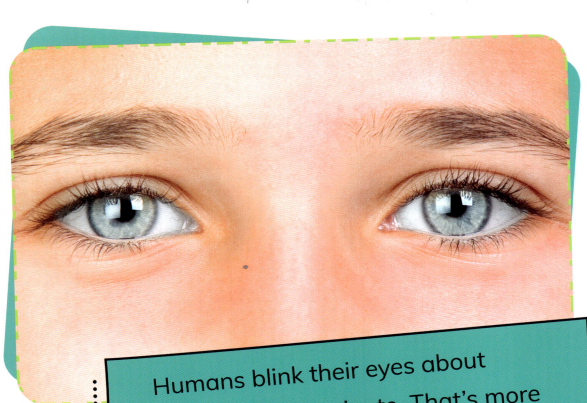

Humans blink their eyes about 20 times every minute. That's more than 200,000 times a week!

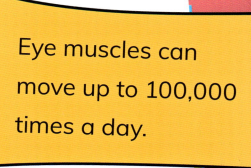

Eye muscles can move up to 100,000 times a day.

Breathing

Humans need to breathe in **oxygen**. We breathe out a gas called **carbon dioxide**. The diaphragm is the muscle we use for breathing.

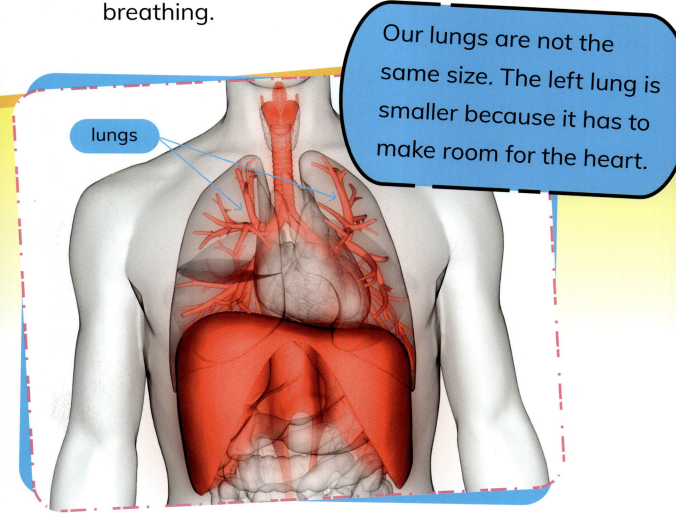

lungs

Our lungs are not the same size. The left lung is smaller because it has to make room for the heart.

When resting, adults breathe between 12 and 20 times per minute.

Chapter 4

The brain and nerves

The brain is part of the nervous system. It sends and receives information from the rest of your body. The main parts of the brain are the cerebrum, the cerebellum and the brain stem.

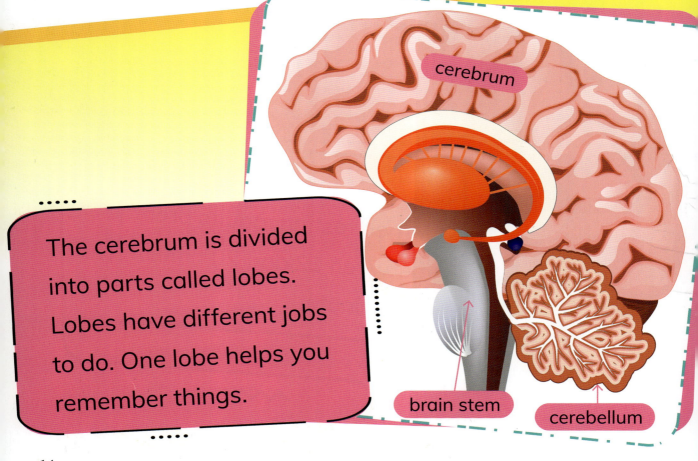

cerebrum

brain stem

cerebellum

The cerebrum is divided into parts called lobes. Lobes have different jobs to do. One lobe helps you remember things.

Cerebellum means "little brain" in Latin. It controls movement.

The brain stem is only about 7.6 centimetres (3 inches) long. It controls movements such as swallowing food.

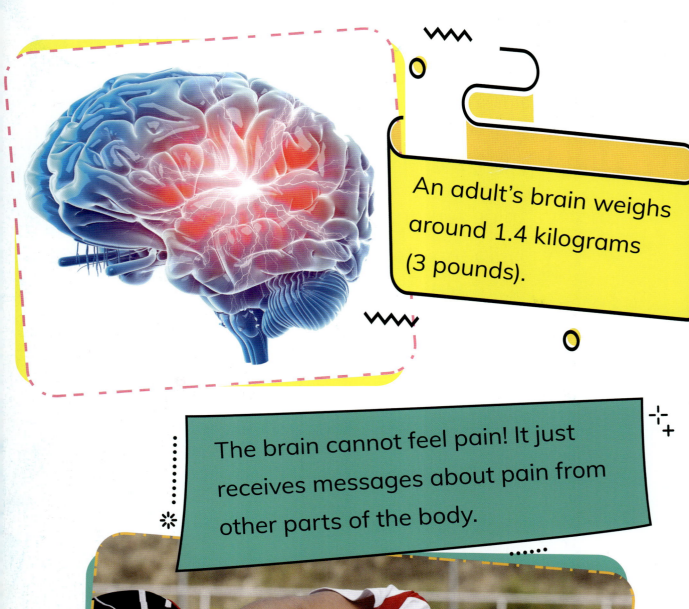

An adult's brain weighs around 1.4 kilograms (3 pounds).

The brain cannot feel pain! It just receives messages about pain from other parts of the body.

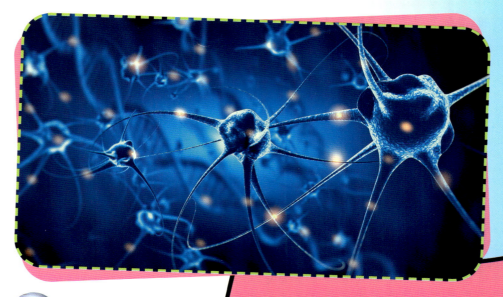

Information is moved around the body by **nerve** cells – at up to 400 km (250 miles) per hour!

The human body has 74 km (46 miles) of nerves!

Chapter 5

Bones

A skeleton supports and shapes our bodies. It is made up of bones.

Adults have 206 bones in their bodies. Babies have about 300. Some of these join together as children grow.

Bones help us to move. They also help to make blood cells and store calcium.

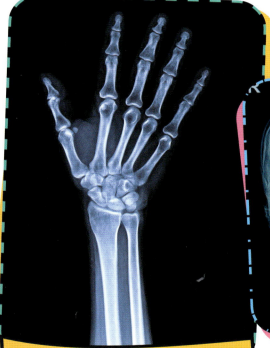

More than half our bones are in our hands and feet!

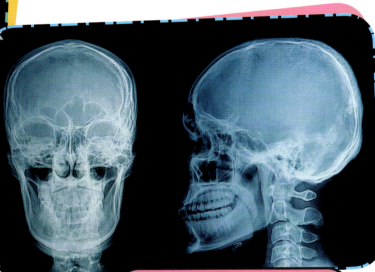

The skull is made up of 22 bones.

There are 33 bones in the spine.
They are shaped like rings. *

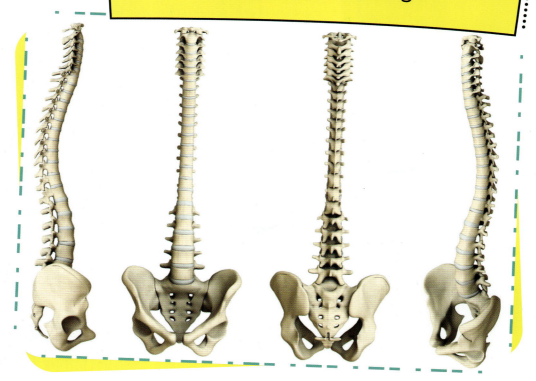

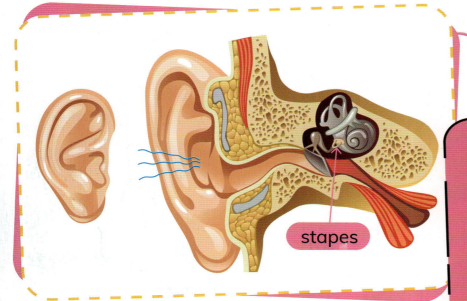

stapes

The stapes is part of the ear. It is the smallest bone in the body.

The largest bone in the body is the femur.

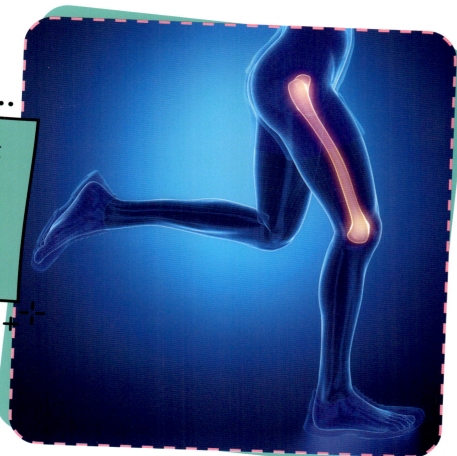

marrow

Bone marrow is like jelly. It is found inside large bones and makes blood cells.

Digestion

Digestion is the way our food gets broken down into parts that are useful for our bodies. We get rid of the parts we don't need when we go to the toilet.

Adults make 1.5 litres (50 fluid ounces) of saliva every day! Saliva helps with digestion.

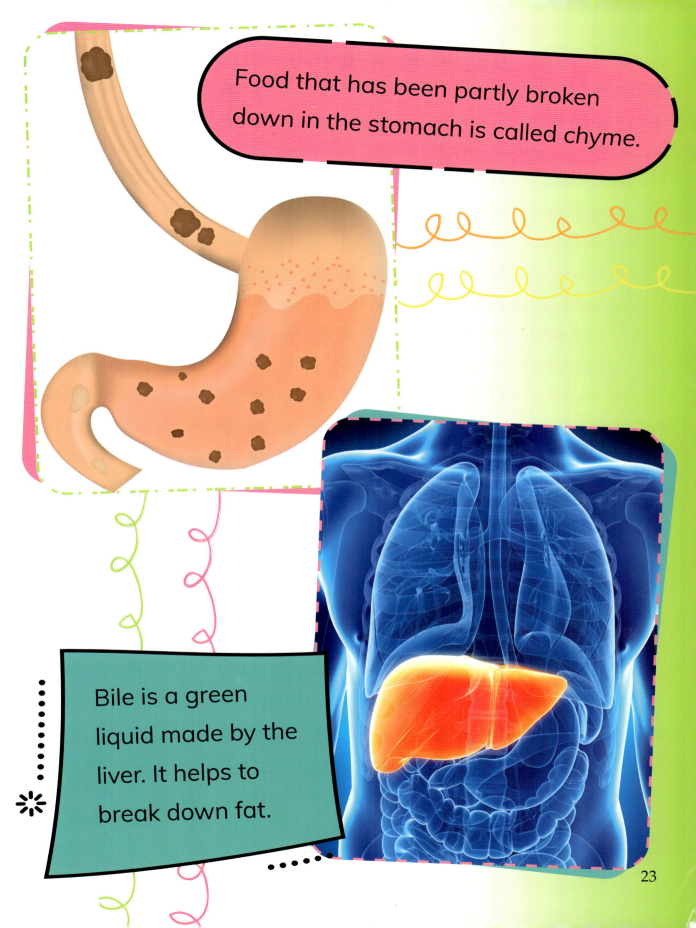

Food that has been partly broken down in the stomach is called chyme.

Bile is a green liquid made by the liver. It helps to break down fat.

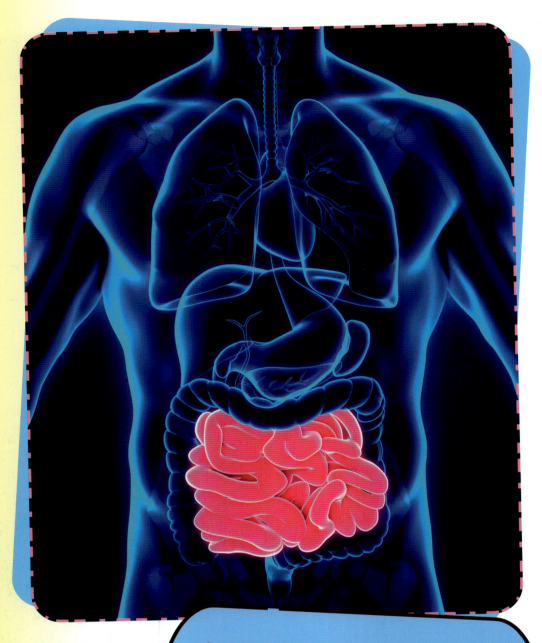

An adult's small intestine isn't small! It measures about 6.7 metres (22 feet) long.

Food can spend about four hours working its way through the small intestine.

Adults make nearly 1.5 litres (50 fluid ounces) of urine every day!

Chapter 7

Senses

Humans have five main senses. These are taste, touch, sight, hearing and smell.

Our noses can recognize more than 1 trillion different smells!

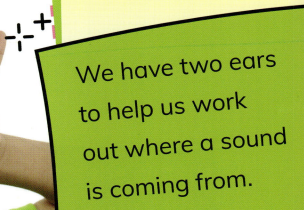

We have two ears to help us work out where a sound is coming from.

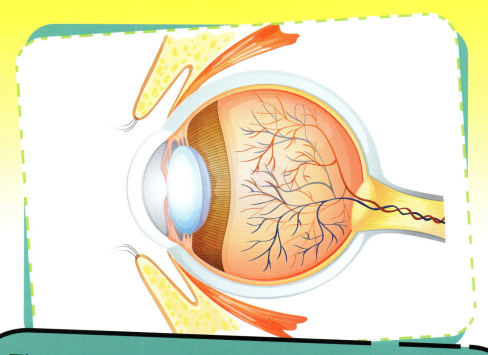

There are cells called rods and cones in the eye. Rods see in black and white. Cones see in colour. Your brain puts them together!

More than three-quarters of what you taste comes from your sense of smell.

Chapter 8

Skin and hair

Our skin and hair help to protect us from diseases. Our skin helps to keep all our bones, **organs** and muscles together.

Skin helps to keep us cool by sweating.

Skin is thicker in some places, such as the bottoms of our feet.

In just one minute, you lose more than 30,000 dead skin cells!

29

The lips, palms of the hands and soles of the feet are the only areas of the body that don't have hair.

We lose 50 to 100 hairs every day.

We have the same number of hairs on our bodies as a chimpanzee! The difference is that our hairs are much thinner and finer.

Once the hair on your head reaches the skin's surface, it is dead. This is why it doesn't hurt to have your hair cut!

Glossary

bone marrow soft jelly-like material in the middle of bones where blood cells are made

carbon dioxide gas with no smell or colour that humans breathe out

cell tiny structure that makes up all living things

nerve thin fibre that carries messages between the brain and other parts of the body

organ body part that does a particular job

oxygen colourless gas that humans need to breathe in to survive

plasma yellow-coloured liquid in blood

platelets tiny, disc-shaped objects that help blood clot and stop bleeding

tendon strong, thick cord of tissue that joins a muscle to a bone

Index